REMOVING THE

'ITES'

FROM YOUR PROMISED LAND

by Dick Bernal

**Jubilee Christian Center
San Jose, California**

Removing the "Ites" From Your Promised Land.

Copyright ©1995 by Dick Bernal

Published by Jubilee Christian Center
San Jose, California 95134

ISBN 1–884920–03–9

Scripture quotations are from The Holy Bible, New King James Version, by Thomas Nelson, Inc.

Printed in the United States of America.

Table of Contents

Introduction

O kay, cop to it. You're frustrated! Things aren't going your way. You're believing with all your believer; you're doing your best to live a good Christian life, but where are the promises? I thought Jesus died so that I could "have life and have it more abundantly." Hey, doesn't the Bible say, "He shall supply all my needs"?

What happened to being the head and not the tail? Or being blessed and not cursed? Is there something so blatantly wrong that God just doesn't like me? Am I reading the Bible correctly or what?

As a pastor and teacher, I get questions like this constantly. I decided to help us all by putting together some food for thought along with a few practical steps on how to possess our Promised Land.

As we all stand on the banks of the Jordan and peer across at God's promises and provisions, let's cross over together and take what is rightfully ours.

Chapter 1

The "Ites" Are Coming!

For all the promises of God in Him are Yes, and in Him Amen, to the Glory of God through us.

2 Corinthians 1:20

God is a God of promises. He keeps His word. He's not fickle, wishy-washy, moody or flaky. James tells us:

> *Every good gift and every perfect gift is from above, and comes down from the Father of lights, with whom there is no variation or shadow of turning.*
>
> James 1:17

From this scripture we get the term, "without a shadow of a doubt." The Bible is often referred to as the "Book of Covenants." A covenant is a promise or contract with rules and regulations. God has His part and we have our part.

Let's take a journey back into the Old Testament and see just how God dealt with His people Israel, especially in the area of conditional promises. The biggest little word in the Bible is "if." Webster tells us "if" means "in the event that" or "on condition that." Here's a good example of what I'm talking about.

> *Now it shall come to pass, if you diligently obey the voice of the Lord your God, to observe carefully all His commandments which I command you today, that the Lord your God will set you high above all nations of the earth.*
>
> Deuteronomy 28:1

God issues a promise but with a condition. "I will if you will!" I like simple theology.

Have you ever heard the terms, "the law of first reference" or "the law of double reference"? Any serious student of the Bible needs to understand these laws.

The law of first reference simply means that God is consistent. He changes not. Once He establishes a principle, it transcends dispen-sation. For example, after the Fall in the Garden of Eden, we read:

> *Also for Adam and his wife the Lord God made tunics of skin, and clothed them.*
>
> Genesis 3:21

Here we see guilty man (woman) being covered (atoned) by a blood sacrifice. A law is enacted. There will be no remission of sin without the shedding of blood—innocent blood covering guilt's sin and shame. This law held fast throughout the ages until Calvary.

Seed time and harvest or sowing and reaping became law as recorded in the book of Genesis and is a law or principle today.

The law of double reference can be referred to as a shadow and type of the new life in Christ.

> *For whatever things were written before were written for our learning, that we through the patience and comfort of the Scriptures might have hope.* Romans 15:4

> *Now all these things happened to them as examples, and they were written for our admonition, upon whom the ends of the ages have come.*   1 Corinthians 10:11

Another word to consider is "example." The double reference or two-edged sword of truth is the literal and the spiritual. Yes, the Old Testament is full of history, literal and factual. And we still learn from these shadows and types. Egypt was a type of the world. Pharaoh, a type of Satan; Moses, a type of Christ; the children of Israel, a type

11

of the Church; the wilderness, a type of mediocre living; Canaan, a type of victory through battle, and so on.

I want to establish this right up front since the purpose of this book is to bring you practical truth. What good is the Bible if we can't work it?

Faith comes by hearing and is released by doing. Let's begin at Exodus 2:23-25.

> *Now it happened in the process of time that the king of Egypt died. Then the children of Israel groaned because of the bondage, and they cried out; and their cry came up to God because of the bondage. So God heard their groaning, and God remembered His covenant with Abraham, with Isaac, and with Jacob. And God looked upon the children of Israel, and God acknowledged them.*

God's covenant (chosen) people are backslid and living in the world (Egypt). Finally they're sick and tired of being tired and sick, so they cry out to God. God hears! However, He's not moved by sentiment, but by promise (covenant).

Several hundred years earlier God made a promise to Abram (Abraham).

> *Now the Lord had said to Abram: "Get out of your country, from your kindred and*

from your father's house, to a land that I
will show you. I will make you a great
nation; I will bless you and make your
name great; and you shall be a blessing. I
will bless those who bless you, and I will
curse him who curses you; and in you all
the families of the earth shall be blessed.

Genesis 12:1-3

The Hebrew people, Abraham's descendants, hit more than just a few speed bumps
on their road to blessing, and eventually
found themselves in bondage.

God finds a deliverer, Moses. In their
inaugural conversation, the Almighty
explains to Moses:

Then He said, "Do not draw near this
place. Take your sandals off your feet, for
the place where you stand is holy ground."
Moreover He said, "I am the God of your
father—the God of Abraham, the God of
Isaac, and the God of Jacob." And Moses
hid his face, for he was afraid to look
upon God.

And the Lord said: "I have surely seen the
oppression of My people who are in Egypt,
and have heard their cry because of their
taskmasters, for I know their sorrows. So I
have come down to deliver them out of the
hand of the Egyptians, and to bring them
up from that land to a good and large
land, to a land flowing with milk and

honey, to the place of the Canaanites and the Hittites and the Amorites and the Perizzites and the Hivites and the Jebusites."

Exodus 3:5-8

God's plan never altered. No Plan B; no shadow of turning.

Notice in verse 8:

- A good land
- A large land
- A land flowing with blessings
- A land full of "Ites."

Yikes! What are "Ites"? Well, they're the people who don't want you to claim your promises, and all God wants to give you. What termites are to wood, the Canaanites are to God's people—a problem! Pesky, destructive and numerous, but if dealt with correctly, they can be eliminated.

Okay, let's get out of Egypt and on with the program. What's the quickest way to the Promised Land, God? I'm ready for a little milk and honey. Oh, not so fast friend. You're no match for what's ahead yet.

Then it came to pass, when Pharaoh had let the people go, that God did not lead them by way of the land of the Philistines, although that was near; for God said,

"Lest perhaps the people change their minds when they see war, and return to Egypt." So God led the people around by way of the wilderness of the Red Sea. And the children of Israel went up in orderly ranks out of the land of Egypt.

Exodus 13:17-18

Remember, it only took a little while to get God's people out of Egypt, but it would take a season to get Egypt out of God's people. Four-hundred years of influence is not easy to shake. These farmers and ranchers who knew nothing but slavery were no match for the warriors of Canaan.

God's people must be discipled. What better place than in the wilderness. Here God will reveal Himself to the children of Israel by His Covenant names. A relationship built on trust must first be established before entering into war.

God sends the Law, establishes church, sets things in order and the training begins. "How long will this take, Lord? I'm craving milk and honey. This ol' desert is kind of dry and boring. I'm ready for the front lines!"

Well, it's going to take as long as it's going to take.

Chapter 2

All Who Are Able, Go To War!

Now the Lord spoke to Moses in the Wilderness of Sinai, in the tabernacle of meeting, on the first day of the second month, in the second year after they had come out of the land of Egypt, saying: "Take a census of all the congregation of the children of Israel, by their families, by their fathers' houses, according to the number of names, every male individually, from twenty years old and above—all who are able to go to war in Israel. You and Aaron shall number them by their armies

Numbers 1:1-3

Now it's time. This mass of confusion coming out of Egypt is becoming an army.

I heard a preacher once say, "First and foremost the church is an army, but it's been reduced to a hospital and a cafeteria."

We as leaders spend most of our time healing, mending and feeding the sheep with precious little time to train for war. The art of making disciples has become the art of just keeping them happy. Dear God, if we don't, they're liable to go to another church and take their friends and money with them. Egad, we can't let that happen, can we?!

All right, we came from the beach to the banks, from the Red Sea to the River Jordan. We've got our BSD degree in theology (Back Side of the Desert), and here we are, just a few yards from Canaanland—the land of promise.

> *And the Lord spoke to Moses, saying, "Send men to spy out the land of Canaan, which I am giving to the children of Israel; from each tribe of their fathers you shall send a man, every one a leader among them." So Moses sent them from the Wilderness of Paran according to the command of the Lord, all of them men who were heads of the children of Israel.*
> Numbers 13:1-3

> *"And see what the land is like: whether the people who dwell in it are strong or weak, few or many; whether the land they dwell in is good or bad; whether the cities they inhabit are like camps or strongholds; whether the land is rich or*

poor; and whether there are forests there or not. Be of good courage. And bring some of the fruit of the land." Now the time was the season of the first ripe grapes. So they went up and spied out the land from the Wilderness of Zin as far as Rehob, near the entrance of Hamath

Numbers 13:18-21

This is good strategy. Look before you leap. There's no such thing as blind faith. Faith needs to be focused—a clear 20/20 vision. It likes to see clearly what it's laying hold of. So far so good. Everything is under control. Forty days pass. The number forty is the number of testing. The spies are going to score an "F."

So they departed and came back to Moses and Aaron and all the congregation of the children of Israel in the Wilderness of Paran, at Kadesh; they brought back word to them and to all the congregation, and showed them the fruit of the land.

Then they told him, and said: "We went to the land where you sent us. It truly flows with milk and honey, and this is its fruit. Nevertheless the people who dwell in the land are strong; the cities are fortified and very large; moreover we saw the descendants of Anak there. The Amalekites dwell in the land of the South; the Hittites, the Jebusites, and the Amorites dwell in the

19

mountains; and the Canaanites dwell by
the sea and along the banks of the
Jordan."

Numbers 13:26-29

"Yes, Moses, the land is everything the Lord
told you it was, including all the "Ites." In
fact there are more "Ites" than we thought
there were, and some of them are very
large. Moses, this is suicide to think we can
evict these people. We look like
grasshoppers compared to them."

But the men who had gone up with him
said, "We are not able to go up against the
people, for they are stronger than we."

Numbers 13:31

Isn't it amazing how bad news travels faster
than the speed of light. Wait a minute.
What's the problem? God knows the giants
are there. The "Ites" have been there for
centuries. They're no match for God and
God's people. But Caleb stayed in faith.

Then Caleb quieted the people before
Moses, and said, "Let us go up at once
and take possession, for we are well able
to overcome it."

Numbers 13:30

But Joshua the son of Nun and Caleb the
son of Jephunneh, who were among those
who had spied out the land, tore their
clothes; and they spoke to all the

congrega-tion of the children of Israel, saying: "The land we passed through to spy out is an exceedingly good land. If the Lord delights in us, then He will bring us into this land and give it to us, 'a land which flows with milk and honey.' Only do not rebel against the Lord, nor fear the people of the land, for they are our bread; their protection has departed from them, and the Lord is with us. Do not fear them."

Numbers 14:6-9

Fear is a powerful force. Fear carries torment and despair. Fear has gripped God's army. They're not going anywhere. At least not in God's direction.

So all the congregation lifted up their voices and cried, and the people wept that night. And all the children of Israel murmured against Moses and Aaron, and the whole congregation said to them, "If only we had died in the land of Egypt! Or if only we had died in this wilderness! Why has the Lord brought us to this land to fall by the sword, that our wives and children should become victims? Would it not be better for us to return to Egypt?" So they said to one another, "Let us select a leader and return to Egypt."

Numbers 14:1-4

Let us select a new pastor and go back to the old way. How dare he try to get us to fight? If God wants us to be blessed, He'll just bless us. We don't have to risk our lives to have church. Hey, what's so wrong with the wilderness anyway? We've got each other, church, manna, quail, water out of rocks, a cloud by day to cool us and a pillar of fire by night to warm us, and let's not forget that our clothes aren't even wearing out. This ain't so bad now, is it! And we don't have to face a bunch of "Ites" and get all caught up in this warfare stuff, do we? Surely God will meet us where we are and be satisfied. What does He expect from us anyway? We're only human!

God has a word with Moses about all this.

> *Then the Lord said to Moses: "How long will these people reject Me? And how long will they not believe Me, with all the signs which I have performed among them? I will strike them with the pestilence and disinherit them, and I will make of you a nation greater and mightier than they."*
> Numbers 14:11-12

Whoops! God doesn't always do what we want Him to do, does He? He's hot! Really upset! Big time ticked! God is a man of war.

> *The Lord is a man of war; the Lord is His name.*   Exodus 15:3

God is not a pacifist, a bleeding heart liberal, nor is He a member of a peace movement (yet). He didn't burn His draft card and run for the Canadian border when war broke out in heaven.

> *And war broke out in heaven: Michael and his angels fought against the dragon; and the dragon and his angels fought, but they did not prevail, nor was a place found for them in heaven any longer. So the great dragon was cast out, that serpent of old, called the Devil and Satan, who deceives the whole world; he was cast to the earth, and his angels were cast out with him.*
>
> Revelation 12:7-9

Many Christians today seem to have a fuzzy, syrupy image of God. Of all His Covenant names, the Lord of Hosts (army) is the most often recorded.

You and I were born into a conflict. We didn't ask to be; it just happened.

Good versus evil.

Light versus darkness.

Right versus wrong.

Is it any wonder Paul used so many military terms to describe spiritual truth: weapons, armor, the good fight, strongholds, swords, wrestling, to name a few.

Let's go back to Numbers 14. Here's the word of the Lord to the rebellious, the wimpy, the backslidden:

> *"But as for you, your carcasses shall fall in this wilderness. And your sons shall be shepherds in the wilderness forty years, and bear the brunt of your infidelity, until your carcasses are consumed in the wilderness. According to the number of the days in which you spied out the land, forty days, for each day you shall bear your guilt one year, namely forty years, and you shall know My rejection. I the Lord have spoken this. I will surely do so to all this evil congregation who are gathered together against Me. In this wilderness they shall be consumed, and there they shall die."*
>
> *Now the men whom Moses sent to spy out the land, who returned and made all the congregation murmur against him by bringing a bad report of the land, those very men who brought the evil report about the land, died by the plague before the Lord.* Numbers 14:32-37

I feel this is a good place to insert Hebrews 10:35-39.

Therefore do not cast away your confidence, which has great reward. For you have need of endurance, so that after you have done the will of God, you may receive the promise: "For yet a little while, and He who is coming will come and will not tarry. Now the just shall live by faith; but if anyone draws back, My soul has no pleasure in him." But we are not of those who draw back to perdition, but of those who believe to the saving of the soul.

Perdition simply means destruction. Why is it people think by quitting on God, church and commitment that life will be easier? "It's too hard to be a Christian," they say. No friend, it's very hard not to be one.

Numbers 33 is an interesting chapter. It chronicles the travels of God's rebellious church. Notice as you read it how many times they camped and moved. Have you ever seen a map of the journeys in the wilderness? For forty years the children of Israel went absolutely nowhere! The reason they camped so many times was to bury their dead. Many of the places they camped were named after their anguish. It doesn't pay to disobey.

One great lesson learned from chapter 33 is that life with God is always on the move.

Just as the Israelites got comfortable in their new camp, the cloud moved. Today we see many camps, tribes, denominations and groups so set in their doctrines and ways that getting them to break camp and move is tough. But the one thing that seems to be motivating a worldwide unity movement is spiritual warfare.

In the wilderness the twelve tribes camped around the tabernacle. The Bible tells us each tribe was unique and had its own standards.

> *And the Lord spoke to Moses and Aaron, saying: "Everyone of the children of Israel shall camp by his own standard, beside the emblems of his father's house; they shall camp some distance from the tabernacle of meeting."*

> Numbers 2:1-2

The twelve tribes of Israel had their own "fathers" (leaders), gifting and style. They were as unique as the Baptists, Pentecostals and Methodists are today.

At times the tribes fussed and squabbled at each other, but when the nation came under attack, the tribes united in war. This is a great lesson for us today. Let's enjoy our differences, style and methods of ministry instead of getting upset with people who don't believe exactly the way our tribe believes. The time is coming, if it's not here already, when our need for each other will far outweigh our petty differences.

Chapter 3

When You Have Crossed the Jordan...

Now the Lord spoke to Moses in the plains of Moab by the Jordan, across from Jericho, saying, "Speak to the children of Israel, and say to them: 'When you have crossed the Jordan into the land of Canaan, then you shall drive out all the inhabitants of the land from before you, destroy all their engraved stones, destroy all their molded images, and demolish all their high places; you shall dispossess the inhabitants of the land and dwell in it, for I have given you the land to possess. And you shall divide the land by lot as an inheritance among your families; to the larger you shall give a larger inheritance, and to the smaller you shall give a smaller inheritance; there everyone's inheritance shall be whatever falls to him by lot. You shall inherit according to the tribes of your fathers. But if you do not drive out the inhabitants of the land from before you, then it shall be that those whom you let remain shall be irritants

in your eyes and thorns in your sides, and
they shall harass you in the land where you
dwell. Moreover it shall be that I will do to
you as I thought to do to them

Numbers 33:50-56

Notice, God does not say *if* you cross over, but *when* you cross over. Most Chris-tians have only one crossing in them. They'll cross over the Red Sea but balk at the Jordan. Just stay in the wilderness and exist. We've settled for the mediocre in place of the good and the great. But God's not through. He's not throwing in the towel. The Joshua people are in the wings and they're ready.

Oh yeah, the "Ites" are still there; in fact probably stronger than ever, but no matter. There's a new spirit of faith in the land.

After the death of Moses the servant of the Lord, it came to pass that the Lord spoke to Joshua the son of Nun, Moses' assistant, saying:

"Moses My servant is dead. Now therefore, arise, go over this Jordan, you and all this people, to the land which I am giving to them—the children of Israel. Every

30

place that the sole of your foot will tread
upon I have given you, as I said to Moses."
Joshua 1:1-3

Moses is dead! It's time for a new movement. <u>Sometimes things have to die for new things to spring</u> forth. Jesus tells us this in the story of the seed (see Luke 8:4-15).

In Isaiah Chapter 6 we see that in the year King Uzziah died, Isaiah got a new vision.

> *...I saw the Lord sitting on a throne, high and lifted up, and the train of His robe filled the temple. Above it stood seraphim; each one had six wings: with two he covered his face, with two he covered his feet, and with two he flew. And one cried to another and said: "Holy, holy, holy is the Lord of hosts; The whole earth if full of His glory!" And the posts of the door were shaken by the voice of him who cried out, and the house was filled with smoke. Then I said: "Woe is me, for I am undone! Because I am a man of unclean lips, and I dwell in the midst of a people of unclean lips; For my eyes have seen the King, the Lord of hosts."* Isaiah 6:1-5

Of course this principle of death giving way to new life is best seen in the death of our Lord and what that birthed.

"Moses my servant is dead; now arise and go...." The Lord is telling Joshua to go, refresh your vision. As one of the original twelve spies in Numbers 13, Joshua saw the Promised Land but that was forty years earlier. You can lose your dream over that long period of time. See it again, Joshua. Get it inside of you! See it so you can believe it. Then believe it so you can see it.

The Lord begins to encourage the new leader.

> *No man shall be able to stand before you all the days of your life; as I was with Moses, so I will be with you. I will not leave you nor forsake you. Be strong and of good courage, for to this people you shall divide as an inheritance the land which I swore to their fathers to give them. Only be strong and very courageous, that you may observe to do according to all the law which Moses My servant commanded you; do not turn from it to the right hand or to the left, that you may prosper wherever you go. This Book of the Law shall not depart from your mouth, but you shall meditate in it day and night, that you may observe to do according to all that is written in it. For then you will make your way prosperous, and then you will have good success.*
>
> Joshua 1:5-8

- Don't be afraid.
- I'll be with you.
- Stay in the Word.
- You'll succeed!

Now when God told Joshua, "I will be with you as I was with Moses," we need to qualify this a bit. The wilderness movement was dead. It died with Moses. No more free lunch. Manna wasn't going to fall from heaven in the Promised Land. No more pillar of fire, cloud by day, water from rocks, sandals that lasted forty years. From now on, God's people would have to fight for what was rightfully theirs, but the Lord would be with them in the battle, if they obeyed.

Chapter 4

The Seven "Ites"

When the Lord your God brings you into the land which you go to possess, and has cast out many nations before you, the Hittites and the Girgashites and the Amorites and the Canaanites and the Perizzites and the Hivites and the Jebusites, seven nations greater and mightier than you, and when the Lord your God delivers them over to you, you shall conquer them and utterly destroy them. You shall make no covenant with them nor show mercy to them. Nor shall you make marriages with them. You shall not give your daughter to their son, nor take their daughter for your son. For they will turn your sons away from following Me, to serve other gods; so the anger of the Lord will be aroused against you and destroy you suddenly.

But thus you shall deal with them: you shall destroy their altars, and break down their sacred pillars, and cut down their wooden images, and burn their carved images with fire. For you are a holy people to the Lord your God; the Lord your God has chosen you to be a people for Himself, a special treasure above all the peoples on the face of the earth. The Lord did not set His love on you nor choose you because you were more in number than any other people, for you were the least of all peoples; but because the Lord loves you, and because He would keep the oath which He swore to your fathers, the Lord has brought you out with a mighty hand, and redeemed you from the house of bondage, from the hand of Pharaoh king of Egypt. Therefore know that the Lord your God, He is God, the faithful God who keeps covenant and mercy for a thousand generations with those who love Him and keep His commandments.

Deuteronomy 7:1-9

H ere we see the seven enemies of God's people—the "Ites" who are bent on keeping the land of promise for themselves. Notice that the Lord reminds His people the "Ites" are strong and great. One must be careful not to underestimate the power of the enemy. Paul calls Satan "the god of this world," and the "prince of the power of the air" for good reasons. Our ancient adversary is an evil genius. He's cunning, subtle, wily, clever, opportunistic and relentless. Man is no match for Satan or his cadre.

A famous televangelist recently said, "I thought I could beat the devil because of who I was, but the truth of the matter is that only Jesus in me could defeat him, but I didn't let Him."

This "fallen" preacher is touching on an important point. If the *battle is the Lord's* (2 Chronicles 20:15), then we had better let Him do it His way. If Jesus *disarmed principalities and powers* (Colossians 2:15) and *destroyed the works of the devil* (I John 3:8) once, He surely can do it again in and through you and me.

> *Greater is He that is in you than he that is in the world.*   I John 4:4

Even though God told the Hebrew nation that the "Ites" are mighty, He's assuring them He will be with them in battle. The acid test is, do they really believe that? Is He truly greater than the "gods" of the Promised Land? Can we trust Him? The fiercest battle is always the one between our ears. If that one can be won, the battle between the Jordan and the Great Sea is a given!

Recently I played a round of golf with a pastor friend. He hadn't played for quite a while but he was a good player. He had the know-how, but was rusty. As we drove an hour to the club, he began talking himself into a good round. "I'm going to play great today," he told me. "I'm going to relax, keep focused, swing smoothly, keep my head down and follow through." He just kept on preaching to himself all the way to the course. Guess what? He played great! He won the battle of doubt and excuses in his own mind before he made his first swing at hole number one.

He pictured every hole, trap, water hazard, tree and other enemy of a good score as he approached the challenge. "I'll shoot under 80 today," he bragged as we stuck our tees into the first hole. He scored a 76. I won't tell you what I scored. It was a very difficult course. His advantage was that he had seen it before. He knew what he was up against. Likewise, when Joshua was told to cross over, he had an advantage. He had seen the layout of the Promised Land and all its traps, hazards...and "Ites." He knew what he and the people of God were up against.

A friend of mine, Pastor Mike Maiden who ministers in Scottsdale, Arizona, did some research on the seven "Ites" of the Promised Land. He found that each "Ite" had a reputation or a meaning attached to its name. I refer to this as the spirit of the "Ites." The spirit of something lives on even after that "something" is dead and gone. For example, the spirit of Babylon is still around. We read about it in the Book of Revelation. With this in mind let's look at the spirit of the seven "Ites" of Deuteronomy 7. We will take them in no particular order.

1. ***Canaanites.*** *These were merchants and traders, unscrupulous sorts. Greedy and materialistic.*

2. ***Hittites.*** *These were horribly warlike and fierce people. The thought of them would instill fear into one's heart.*

3. ***Hivites.*** *Their name literally means, "to live a lie."*

4. ***Perizzites.*** *Unprotected, open, no walls, nomadic, restless people.*

5. ***Gergashites.*** *Dwellers of the clay or marsh.*

6. ***Amorites.*** *Mountain people, lived above the rest.*

7. ***Jebusites.*** *Trodden down, depressed.*

In these next seven chapters we will look at the spirit of the "Ites" and how we can evict them off our Canaanland—our land of promise and answered prayers.

Chapter 5

<u>Canaanites</u> Spirit of Materialism

If you're around my age you might remember the old tune that had the line, "Money, honey, if you want to get along with me," or the "Big Bopper" and his famous laugh and line, "O Baby, you know what I like . . . MONEY." Money—that strange stuff that turns the world's crank.

Too much of it is dangerous, and so is too little. Where is the balance for the believer? Just how much is too much? Poverty is certainly not God's will, nor is decadence.

Jesus came that we might have life, and have it more abundantly (John 10:10), but where does money come into this, or does it? Are God's blessings only spiritual, or is He also concerned with our natural needs?

We know the scripture,

> *For the love of money is a root of all kinds of evil, for which some have strayed from the faith in their greediness, and pierced themselves through with many sorrows.*
> I Timothy 6:10

Paul did not say that *money* is evil, but our *love* for it is. Money is not immoral, but amoral. It's simply a tool, and what we do with this tool is being, and will be judged.

As a kid I loved the Jack Benny Show. We would all gather around our black and white RCA television set and howl at Jack, Rodchester, Don and Mary. One of my favorite skits had Jack being held up by a thug. The robber said, "Your money or your life!" Jack slowly looked into the camera and asked, "How long do I have to make up my mind?" Sometimes during the offering at Jubilee, I see a few of the same blank expressions as God tries to deliver man from his money. Even though we sit on our wallet, it's still the closest object to our heart.

> *For where your treasure is, there your heart will be also.* Matthew 6:21

Jesus also tells us it's hard for the rich to enter heaven because too often their faith and love are wrapped up in their things. This doesn't pertain to all the rich, but a good majority of them. One very successful businessman approached a famous preacher and told him, "Son, I'd sure like to help your ministry but my money's all tied up." The preacher looked square at him and replied, "Sir, perhaps it's *you* who is all tied up."

One of my favorite courses I teach at our Sierra Pacific Bible College is on *wisdom*. My text is the book of Proverbs which tells us in two-line poems how to live successfully on this planet. The key foundational words besides wisdom are instruction, integrity, discretion, understanding, knowledge, justice, prudence and counsel. Once the foundation is laid, Solomon goes on to talk about the proper use of money. Here's a man who knows money's place. He compares the blessing and the cursing of riches. Basically it depends on the person's heart and attitude towards money.

> *He who has a slack hand becomes poor, but the hand of the diligent makes rich.*
> Proverbs 10:4

> *The spirit of a man will sustain him in sickness, but who can bear a broken spirit? The heart of the prudent acquires knowledge, and the ear of the wise seeks*

knowledge. A man's gift makes room for him, and brings him before great men. The first one to plead his cause seems right, until his neighbor comes and examines him. Casting lots causes contentions to cease, and keeps the mighty apart.

Proverbs 18:14-18

Yet Solomon warns us about trusting in riches in Proverbs 11:27-28:

He who diligently seeks good finds favor, but trouble will come to him who seeks evil. He who trusts in his riches will fall, but the righteous will flourish like foliage.

When I give my yearly teaching on "Giving as Worship," I always touch on Jesus' parable in Luke 16:1-13:

And He also said to His disciples: "There was a certain rich man who had a steward, and an accusation was brought to him that this man was wasting his goods. So he called him and said to him, 'What is this I hear about you? Give an account of your stewardship, for you can no longer be steward.'

"Then the steward said within himself, 'What shall I do? For my master is taking the stewardship away from me. I cannot dig; I am ashamed to beg. I have resolved what to do, that when I am put out of the

stewardship, they may receive me into their houses.'

"So he called every one of his master's debtors to him, and said to the first, 'How much do you owe my master?' And he said, 'A hundred measures of oil.' So he said to him, 'Take your bill, and sit down quickly and write fifty.'

"Then he said to another, 'And how much do you owe?' So he said, 'A hundred measures of wheat.' And he said to him, 'Take your bill, and write eighty.'

"So the master commended the unjust steward because he had dealt shrewdly. For the sons of this world are more shrewd in their generation than the sons of light.

"And I say to you, make friends for yourselves by unrighteous mammon, that when you fail, they may receive you into everlasting habitations. He who is faithful in what is least is faithful also in much; and he who is unjust in what is least is unjust also in much.

"Therefore if you have not been faithful in the unrighteous mammon, who will commit to your trust the true riches? And if you have not been faithful in what is another man's, who will give you what is your own?

> *"No servant can serve two masters; for either he will hate the one and love the other or else he will be loyal to the one and despise the other. You cannot serve God and mammon."*

At a surface glance one might scratch his head and wonder at the words of Jesus.

- The unjust steward is being commended?

- Make friends with unrighteous mammon?

- When you fail?

- The sons of the world are more shrewd than the sons of light?

We should note that the three preceding parables were spoken to the Pharisees, but this one was spoken to His disciples (us).

This little story is not as complex or mysterious as some commentators would lead us to believe. The "dramatic personae" are not numerous. Here's a wealthy landowner who has an embezzler as a steward or manager. It's not that the steward was inept, but rather irresponsible; a squanderer of his master's goods. He's busted and given notice of termination. The man panics! "Oh my, what to do? I'm above digging ditches and too proud to beg." What a prince of a guy!

He cleverly comes up with a solution. Before news spreads of his dismissal, he makes friends at his boss' expense. He cuts a couple of deals to insure his life after employment. In verse 8, he gets caught again by his master, but this time he gets a different response. The master tips his hat to his ex-manager for his cleverness. "You little son of a gun; you got me again." (D.B. Version!)

Maybe the landowner got a good laugh at it. Perhaps the rich man got his wealth the same way and it was pay-back time. The steward still got fired but made provision for himself along the way. He knew how to work the world's system—a system that's corrupt, lustful, greedy and absolutely without principle. An unrighteous system that works for the unrighteous. One where lying, cheating and backbiting is the ladder to the top. Halfway through verse 8, Jesus looks at his own followers and says, "For the children of this world are more shrewd in their generation than the sons of light (church people)." Ouch! What a rebuke.

What's behind this saying of His? Actually it's quite simple. The world has a system and 100 percent of the world's people play the game. Some play it better than others and so they prosper. God's kingdom has a system. It's called tithes and offerings, yet less than 20 percent of His sons work the system. We seem to have more confidence in Dow Jones than in Jesus Christ! Our security and investments feel better to us in the world's soil than in heaven's.

The unjust steward worked his system and his system worked for him. We seem to be somewhat confused. Jesus tells us, "Make friends with money" (verse 9). Yes, even with the world's money or "mammon." How does one make friends with money? By putting it in the hands of God.

Our Lord goes on to say if we can't be faithful with money, paying our bills, tithes, vows, etc., how then can we expect God Almighty to entrust us with true riches? What are true riches? Spiritual gifts, ministry gifts, anointings, favor, just to name a few. It never ceases to amaze me how flaky people desire spiritual power.

In verse 13 our Lord gets real strong. In essence He is saying to us, the Church, if you're not willing to give to God, yet you call yourself a Christian, you're a liar. You are the worst kind of hypocrite. The only reasons you're not giving are your fear of lack, and love of self. Giving is worship.

- Who do we love?

- Who do we serve?

- Who do we worship?

To me the whole thing about Christians and money can be settled in Deuteronomy 8:17-18:

> ...then you say in your heart, "My power and the might of my hand have gained me this wealth." And you shall remember the Lord your God, for it is He who gives you power to get wealth, that He may establish His covenant which He swore to your fathers, as it is this day.

I don't think God is all that concerned with our houses, cars, clothes or food. Let's live according to our means and conscience, but keep our eyes on the big picture. The world patiently waits for the gospel.

Spirit of Materialism—be bound in Jesus' Name!

Chapter 6

Hittites
Spirit of Fear

The Hittites were a gnarly bunch. The very name brought a chill down the spine of a brave Hebrew, yet to take the land of promise, the Hittites had to be dealt with. No skirting around the issue. Fear would have to be conquered for victory to come.

"Fear not!" These are two of the most widely used words in the whole Bible. Why is fear such a problem? It's like our reactions to a neighbor we've had for years. . . one we don't like but have gotten used to anyway. Fear is an emotion that is all too familiar. Perhaps Adam can be blamed. It was his first response to the Fall in the garden.

> *Then the Lord God called to Adam and said to him, "Where are you?" So he said, "I heard Your voice in the garden, and I*

was afraid because I was naked; and I hid myself."   Genesis 3:9-10

Fear is faith's greatest obstacle for it breeds doubt, torment, confusion, doublemindedness, flight and hate. Besides these, it fosters the greatest sin found in the church today—compromise. The Berkeley Reference Dictionary says fear is: "Alarm and agitation caused by expectation or realization of danger. To be frightened, to suspect, timid, to be apprehensive."

There is of course another fear which is healthy—the fear of the Lord. The Bible commands us to have it. *The fear of the Lord is the beginning of knowledge.* (Proverbs 1:7) Here the word "fear" speaks of reverence, awe and respect. Both fears motivate. One pushes away; the other draws to.

The negative kind of fear is one great big stop sign on your road to destiny. Fear is the dread of losing something...

- your precious life

- your things

- your reputation

- maybe a relationship

- your money

Fear has driven people to do crazy things, even commit murder or suicide.

Fear takes no chances; it reasons away victory; it looks for the easy way out; it seeks the comfort zone.

Is it any wonder that we are to pray daily for boldness and courage? I personally know the gut-wrenching feeling of fear. It grips one's soul like a cold, steel vice and slowly tries to squeeze all the strength out. More than once over the last 15 years of pastoring, I have woken up in a cold sweat worrying about all that could go wrong.

Fear's best friend is worry. Worry is the constant rehearsing of all that could possibly go wrong. I don't know how many times I've turned on my night-light and opened the book of Psalms to fellowship a little with my friend, King David. As I read of his agony and distress in times of trouble, I track with him to victory in God. It's amazing the strength that leaps off the pages of Holy Writ.

> *For God has not given us a spirit of fear, but of power and of love and of a sound mind.* 2 Timothy 1:7

> *There is no fear in love; but perfect love casts out fear, because fear involves*

torment. But he who fears has not been made perfect in love. 1 John 4:18

Be strong and of good courage, for to this people you shall divide as an inheritance the land which I swore to their fathers to give them. Only be strong and very courageous, that you may observe to do according to all the law which Moses My servant commanded you; do not turn from it to the right hand or to the left, that you may prosper wherever you go.

This Book of the Law shall not depart from your mouth, but you shall meditate in it day and night, that you may observe to do according to all that is written in it. For then you will make your way prosperous, and then you will have good success.

Joshua 1:6-9

Spirit of Fear—be bound in *Jesus*' name!

Chapter 7

Hivites
Spirit of
Compromise and
Deception

What's worse than lying? It's to live a lie and believe it to be the truth. The Bible tells us the devil has deceived the whole world. The world here speaks of those outside the Body of Christ. The masses of blind humanity are being led by false religions, hopes and dreams, all based on a lie.

> *...whose minds the god of this age has blinded, who do not believe, lest the light of the gospel of the glory of Christ, who is the image of God, should shine on them.*
> 2 Corinthians 4:4

So the great dragon was cast out, that serpent of old, called the Devil and Satan, who deceives the whole world; he was cast to the earth, and his angels were cast out with him.   Revelation 12:9

To be deceived is to be misled, tricked, duped or fooled. Here's a scripture that typifies the epitome of deception from Jeremiah 7:8-16:

"Behold, you trust in lying words that cannot profit. Will you steal, murder, commit adultery, swear falsely, burn incense to Baal, and walk after other gods whom you do not know, and then come and stand before Me in this house which is called by My name, and say, 'We are delivered to do all these abominations'?

"Has this house, which is called by My name, become a den of theives in your eyes? Behold, I, even I, have seen it, says the Lord. But go now to My place which was in Shiloh, where I set My name at the first, and see what I did to it because of the wickedness of My people Israel. And now, because you have done all these works, says the Lord, and I spoke to you, rising up early and speaking, but you did not hear, and I called you, but you did not answer, therefore I will do to this house which is called by My name, in which you trust, and to this place which I gave to

you and your fathers, as I have done to Shiloh. And I will cast you out of My sight, as I have cast out all your brethren—the whole posterity of Ephraim. Therefore do not pray for this people, nor lift up a cry or prayer for them, nor make intercession to Me; for I will not hear you."

I've sat in my office and heard stories and fantasies from well-meaning folks and wondered how people could get so far off base and believe they're in God's will. For the most part, they are good people, church people, yet somehow a little deception got in and grew into craziness that everyone could see but them.

I guess we all know what it's like to be fooled; to believe in people who have tricked us. I've been associated with a few slick snakes passing themselves off as spiritual people.

To "change the truth to a lie" takes awhile. Satan likes to spoonfeed small doses of compromise. A little here, a little there, and eventually "the little foxes destroy the vine." Is it any wonder the belt that holds our armor on is called the "belt of truth"? All the other parts hang off truth!

Look at Psalm 1:1-6:

Blessed is the man who walks not in the counsel of the ungodly, nor stands in the path of sinners, nor sits in the seat of the scornful; but his delight is in the law of the Lord, and in His law he meditates day and night. He shall be like a tree planted by the rivers of water, that brings forth its fruit in its season, whose leaf also shall not wither; and whatever he does shall prosper. The ungodly are not so, but are like the chaff which the wind drives away. Therefore the ungodly shall not stand in the judgment, nor sinners in the congregation of the righteous. For the Lord knows the way of the righteous, but the way of the ungodly shall perish.

Notice the sequence—

- Walking

- Standing

- Sitting

Walk not in compromise because if you do, you'll stop, and if you stop, you'll eventually sit.

How many young Christians started their walk right, but compromise crept in and got them off course? Notice the ungodly sinners and the scornful, and avoid them all!

King David wrote Psalm 51 out of brokenness. He had sinned against God by going into Bathsheba and eventuallly having Uriah, her husband, killed. Nathan, the prophet, rebuked the king. David could have lied to save his own hide, blamed others for his sin, or even had Nathan killed for talking to the king that way. But no, David loved God and truth.

Integrity is tested more in bad times than in good times. How you and I handle mistakes will determine how we handle success. When God's instructions are crystal clear, we need not confer with flesh and blood. Everyone has an opinion and they are quick to share it. Counsel is good, but not at the expense of the Royal Command. The Lord rarely chooses the path of least resistance.

- Speak the truth in love
- Walk the walk of truth
- Preach the truth
- Tell the truth
- Fight for truth

Spirit of Compromise and Deception—be bound in Jesus' name!

Chapter 8

**Perizzites** _Spirit of_ _Immorality_

Flee sexual immorality. Every sin that a man does is outside the body, but he who commits sexual immorality sins against his own body. Or do you not know that your body is the temple of the Holy Spirit who is in you, whom you have from God, and you are not your own? For you were bought at a price; therefore glorify God in your body and in your spirit, which are God's.

Now concerning the things of which you wrote to me: It is good for a man not to touch a woman. Nevertheless because of sexual immorality, let each man have his own wife, and let each woman have her own husband. Let the husband render to his wife the affection due her, and likewise also the wife to her husband.

The wife does not have authority over her own body, but the husband does. And *likewise the husband does not have author-ity over his own body, but the wife does. Do not deprive one another except with consent for a time, that you may give yourselves to fasting and prayer; and come together again so that Satan does not tempt you because of your lack of self-control. But I say this as a concession, not as a commandment.*

1 Corinthians 6:18-7:6

Ever notice that sexual sins are talked about more than any other in the Bible? God made us and gave us a sex drive. Sex was not created to be dirty, perverted, flippantly used, a means to get satisfaction, or to be sold. Sex is a celebration of love between covenant mates, not the culmination of lust.

Love gives; lust takes. Love is humble and submissive; lust is arrogant and possessive. Lust is taking one's sex drive and putting it into overdrive. Immorality is not a new phenomenon. It's been around since time (man's time) began. Homosexuality is not a San Francisco invention. It too has been around a long, long time. Venereal diseases of all kinds and perhaps even AIDS aren't new.

The Bible speaks of such things as being a part of the Curse. A recent CNN/*Time* poll said the decline in morality was the number two concern of Americans, right behind violence. Interesting! Maybe America is waking up. The "love-ins" of the 60s and the "anything goes" of the 70s and 80s have soured in our mouths.

> *For the lips of an immoral woman drip honey and her mouth is smoother than oil; but in the end she is bitter as wormwood, sharp as a two-edged sword. Her feet go down to death, her steps lay hold of hell. Lest you ponder her path of life—her ways are unstable; you do not know them.*
> Proverbs 5:3-6

AIDS, abortion-on-demand, rape, children out of wedlock, and an assortment of other sexually-related tragedies are placing a high demand on government dollars, not to mention social trauma. In America, six out of ten marriages end in divorce; many are a result of unfaithfulness. This "Ite" has "done in" many a good preacher, male and female.

This particular stronghold, which seemed to be a worldly problem, has seeped into the church. Paul spoke much about this, especially to the Corinthian church.

It is actually reported that there is sexual immorality among you, and such sexual immorality as is not even named among the Gentiles—that a man has his father's wife! 1 Corinthians 5:1

Foods for the stomach and the stomach for foods, but God will destroy both it and them. Now the body is not for sexual immorality but for the Lord, and the Lord for the body. 1 Corinthians 6:13

Nevertheless, because of sexual immorality, let each man have his own wife, and let each woman have her own husband.

1 Corinthians 7:2

Nor let us commit sexual immorality, as some of them did, and in one day twenty-three thousand fell.

1 Corinthians 10:8

Our senses are bombarded daily with sensual images: billboards, television, movies, music, dress and smell. It's impossible to isolate oneself from all of it, so we must pray for strength daily, or like the Perizzites, our walls will come down and we will be unprotected.

Spirit of Immorality—be bound in Jesus' name!

Chapter 9

Girgashites Spirit of Double-Mindedness

But let him ask in faith, with no doubting, for he who doubts is like a wave of the sea driven and tossed by the wind. For let not that man suppose that he will receive anything from the Lord; he is a double-minded man, unstable in all his ways.

James 1:6-8

I know your works, that you are neither cold nor hot. I could wish you were cold or hot. So then, because you are lukewarm, and neither cold nor hot, I will spew you out of My mouth.   Revelation 3:15-16

T he Girgashites were a type of "gray-area living" church people, living by no real absolutes, no black or white. These folks floundered around in the pastels of life, stuck in the mud without enough sense to know it.

A friend of mine shared a story about a drunk driver who was fleeing from the cops. The drunk lost control of his vehicle and went into the grassy divider of the freeway. Since it had been raining, his tires quickly sank into the mud. The drunk floored the pedal and the back tires simply spun and threw mud everywhere. The cops just watched and laughed until they handcuffed him. The drunk had the accelerator down and the motor was screaming, but he wasn't going anywhere.

> *I waited patiently for the Lord; and He inclined to me, and heard my cry. He also brought me up out of a horrible pit, out of the miry clay, and set my feet upon a rock, and established my steps*

Psalm 40:1-2

The muck and the mire are no place for the believer.

> *For if, after they have escaped the pollutions of the world through the kowledge of the Lord and Savior Jesus Christ, they are again entangled in them and overcome, the latter end is worse for them than the beginning. For it would*

have been better for them not to have known the way of righteousness, than having known it, to turn from the holy commandment delivered to them. But it has happened to them according to the true proverb: "A dog returns to his own vomit," and, "a sow, having washed, to her wallowing in the mire."

2 Peter 2:20-22

Perhaps one's tendency to return to the swamps of life is because our bodies were formed of dust and clay, and with the Adamic nature constantly tempting and suggesting, some do slip. Yet God is always there to rescue us.

Years ago a friend and I were going duck hunting in my 4-wheel drive Ford pick-up. We were almost there when my friend needed to go to the bathroom. We were in the sticks with no gas stations in sight, so I just pulled off the side of the road. Unfortunately, my truck slipped into a ditch. No problem, I thought. I have 4-wheel drive. To my surprise, I couldn't get out. I could go forward and backwards in the wet ditch, but couldn't get out. We tried for two hours, getting more and more frustrated all the time. Finally, my friend walked to a nearby farm and got a man to bring his big tractor and pull us out.

We needed more power than we had to get unstuck. We had some place to go and something to do, so we didn't give up until we got out.

Don't give up. Get out of your ditch.

Spirit of Double-mindedness— be bound in Jesus' name!

Chapter 10

**Amorites**
Spirit of Pride

_And I said to you, You have come to the
mountains of the Amorites, which the
Lord our God is giving us._

Deuteronomy 1:20

The Amorites lived up in the mountains.
According to Pastor Maiden's research
on these people, their very name means
proud, boastful, rebellious mountaineers.
All through the Old Testament, the
Amorites were a real problem to the
Hebrew nation.

_But in the fourth generation they shall
return here, for the iniquity of the
Amorites is not yet complete._

Genesis 15:16

These arrogant dwellers of the Promised
Land had very little respect for the God of
Israel. Too bad they never heard the

scripture, "God resists the proud and gives grace to the humble." (James 4:6b) But the children of God knew all too well how God views pride.

> *I will set My face against you, and you shall be defeated by your enemies. Those who hate you shall reign over you, and you shall flee when no one pursues you. And after all this, if you do not obey Me, then I will punish you seven times more for your sins. I will break the pride of your power; I will make your heavens like iron and your earth like bronze.*
>
> Leviticus 26:17-19

Pride is called the original sin, and it was the main cause of Lucifer's fall.

> *You were perfect in your ways from the day you were created, till iniquity was found in you."*　　Ezekiel 28:15

> *How you are fallen from heaven, O Lucifer, son of the morning! How you are cut down to the ground, you who weakened the nations! For you have said in your heart: "I will ascend into heaven, I will exalt my throne above the stars of God; I will also sit on the mount of the congregation on the farthest sides of the north; I will ascend above the heights of the clouds, I will be like the Most High."*
>
> Isaiah 14:12-14

Pride says—

- I'll do it my way.
- I don't need help.
- I am self-sufficient.
- Get out of my way!

Simply put, pride is self-respect for one's own dignity, honor and worth. Let me share a few proverbs with you:

I, wisdom, dwell with prudence, and find out knowledge and discretion. The fear of the Lord is to hate evil; pride and arrogance and the evil way and the perverse mouth I hate.   Proverbs 8:12-13

Dishonest scales are an abomination to the Lord, but a just weight is His delight. When pride comes, then comes shame; but with the humble is wisdom

Proverbs 11:1-2

By pride comes only contention, but with the well-advised is wisdom

Proverbs 13:10

Pride goes before destruction, and a haughty spirit before a fall

Proverbs 16:18

A man's pride will bring him low, but the humble in spirit will retain honor.

Proverbs 29:23

Years ago I heard a television preacher boast that he was the only one preaching the whole truth. Not much later he fell and never recovered. Recently a friend and I were attending a minister's conference. A young, up and coming minister was firing away, taking pot shots at the faith movement, worship, spiritual warfare, and anyone or anything else that wasn't from his camp. My friend leaned over and whispered, "A couple of failures will humble that boy and he'll be great as he grows."

> • Pride tells us we're right and others are wrong.
>
> • Pride tells us we can sin and get away with it.
>
> • Pride tells us we have to have more, bigger, faster, greater.
>
> • Pride tells us to rejoice in our brother's problems.
>
> • Pride tells us don't forgive.

Of the seven things the Lord hates the most in Proverbs 6:16-19, pride is number one.

John warns us in 1 John 2:15-17:

> *Do not love the world or the things in the world. If anyone loves the world, the love of the Father is not in him. For all that is in the world—the lust of the flesh, the lust*

of the eyes, and the pride of life—is not of the Father but is of the world. And the world is passing away, and the lust of it; but he who does the will of God abides forever.

Spirit of Pride—be bound in Jesus name!

Chapter 11

Jebusites <u></u>
Spirit of Depression

Here we meet and defeat the last of the seven "Ites." Depression left unchecked will lead to discouragement, despair and condemnation.

I read recently the results of a poll taken in *Newsweek* magazine indicating that one-third of all Americans are depressed, and the number of women who are depressed is on the rise. Church people are not exempt from this attack.

Life is a constant battle. Look at the many Vietnam Vets wandering our city streets, depressed, mentally fatigued or battle weary. Far too many of God's army have low self-esteem, weak faith, and battle condem-nation daily.

A favorite verse of mine is Galatians 6:9:

And let us not grow weary while doing good, for in due season we shall reap if we do not lose heart.

Many heroes of faith fought through depression and condemnation. Moses, Joshua, David, Elijah, Isaiah, Jeremiah and of course Peter, all had their down times.

Then Joshua tore his clothes, and fell to the earth on his face before the ark of the Lord until evening, both he and the elders of Israel; and they put dust on their heads. And Joshua said, "Alas, Lord God, why have You brought this people over the Jordan at all—to deliver us into the hand of the Amorites, to destroy us? Oh, that we had been content, and dwelt on the other side of the Jordan!

"O Lord, what shall I say when Israel turns its back before its enemies? For the Canaanites and all the inhabitants of the land will hear it, and surround us, and cut off our name from the earth. Then what will You do for Your great name?" So the Lord said to Joshua: "Get us! Why do you lie thus on your face?"

Joshua 7:6-10

So David and his men came to the city, and there it was, burned with fire; and their wives, their sons, and their daughters had been taken captive. Then David and the people who were with him

76

lifted up their voices and wept, until they had no more power to weep. And David's two wives, Ahinoam the Jezreelitess, and Abigail the widow of Nabal the Carmelite, had been taken captive. Then David was greatly distressed, for the people spoke of stoning him, because the soul of all the people was grieved, every man for his sons and his daughters. But David strengthened himself in the Lord his God.

1 Samuel 30:3-6

And Ahab told Jezebel all that Elijah had done, also how he had executed all the prophets with the sword. Then Jezebel sent a messenger to Elijah, saying, "So let the gods do to me, and more also, if I do not make your life as the life of one of them by tomorrow about this time."

And when he saw that, he arose and ran for his life, and went to Beersheba, which belongs to Judah, and left his servant there. But he himself went a day's journey into the wilderness, and came and sat down under a broom tree. And he prayed that he might die, and said, "It is enough! Now, Lord, take my life, for I am no better than my fathers!"   1 Kings 19:1-4

The problem with condemnation is that it feels a lot like conviction. Both have drawing power. Condemnation draws you away from God while conviction draws you to God. One is designed to destroy; the other to save.

Depression kills. . .

> vision,
>
> hope,
>
> strength,
>
> zeal,
>
> and joy.

The literal meaning of Jebusite is "trodden down." The devil wants to walk all over us, then stomp us into an early grave.

Recently a good friend of Carla's and mine committed suicide. He was a very successful surgeon who appeared to have little want. He was a leader in his church and seemed content in life. He had mentioned his struggles with depression several years earlier, but said he was doing much better now. Two months later he took his life. To this day we still shake our heads in disbelief. Why? Could we have helped? Was he reaching out to us? We almost let his depression rub off on us.

In 1984 I had a miserable bout with depression. I laid on my couch for a week, with thoughts of leaving the ministry. "It's too hard!" "Who needs all this grief!" "Who cares, anyway?" Boy, I had a "Job-type" of a pity party. My wife and a preacher friend encouraged me until I was back on my feet again. Today it's hard to get me down; I just don't let my guard down.

> *There is therefore now no condemnation to those who are in Christ Jesus, who do not walk according to the flesh, but according to the Spirit. For the law of the Spirit of life in Christ Jesus has made me free from the law of sin and death. For what the law could not do in that it was weak through the flesh, God did by sending His own Son in the likeness of sinful flesh, on account of sin: He condemned sin in the flesh*

> Romans 8:1-3

Spirit of Depression—be bound in Jesus' name!

Conclusion

There they are! The seven "Ites" God warned the children of Israel about. Seven enemies that had to be dealt with before full victory could be enjoyed—

- Materialism
- Fear
- Compromise
- Immorality
- Double-mindedness
- Pride
- Depression

Any one of the seven can knock us out of the race or push us back into the wilderness.

We are to know our enemy. I pray that this little book has helped you to identify and locate hinderances to your walk so you can bind them forever in Jesus' name. God created each of us to be a success and to be a winner. Let's do it together.

Other Books by Dick Bernal

America Spiritually Mapped	$9.95
When Lucifer and Jezebel Join Your Church	$6.95
Questions God Asks	$5.95
Who Is God? What Is Man?	$6.95
Curses: What They Are and How to Break Them	$6.95
Come Down Dark Prince	$4.95

* * *

<u>Coming Soon!</u>

Lifting Him Up

by Dick Bernal and Ron Kenoly

* * *

Available through
Jubilee Christian Center
175 Nortech Parkway
San Jose, CA 95134
(408) 262-0900